T0147126

Once
Addicted
NOW SAVED

BILL SMITH

BALBOA.
PRESS

A DIVISION OF HAY HOUSE

Balboa Press books may be ordered through booksellers or by contacting:

Balboa Press
A Division of Hay House
1663 Liberty Drive
Bloomington, IN 47403
www.balboapress.com.au
1 (877) 407-4847

Print information available on the last page.

ISBN: 978-1-5043-0023-0 (sc)
ISBN: 978-1-5043-0024-7 (e)

Balboa Press rev. date: 12/02/2015

Hello this is my story my name is bill smith born 12/05/57 at sydney hospital we lived at five dock opposite the river with my mum and dad and grandfather. Till the age of 2 and mum and dad bought a block of land. And had a house built on it,my dad worked on the wharfs. I began school at public school. To 6th class when I was 7 years old I used to go to work with my dad.He ran a engine room that was to operate press machine up stairs on the wharfs compress bales of wool. It was great fun I used to climb over the piles wool. I remember one year dad made me a yacht,told me to stay in engine room. And when he came back we would go and sail it. I waited about 5 minutes until he was gone went out to sail it. And I fell in the harbour and couldn't swim it was only that I had new school shoe on,to brake in and I kicked my legs. And there was a ship just arrived and a tug boat at bow they came over,pulled me out of the water. And took me to the first aid room half way along the wharf. And I new I was in trouble, in the mean time dad's looking everywhere for me. Wharfie told dad were I was. You guessed it I got a hiding never done it again. I started sunday school at 7 years old went till I was 12,I was a normal kid growing up. Loved riding my bike swimming in our pool. Playing football loved going fishing with mum and dad.Playing in the creek with my friends, we used to get milk bottle tops and use them as little boats and float them down the creek.I had fun times as a kid of a weekend mum dad and myself. Would pack the car and head to beach on the north shore, loved body surfing floating around on my float. And just enjoying our time together as a family. Mum would pack a lunch we had the picnic table dad and I would set that up. Then when we got back home we would go for a swim in our pool wash the salt off, they were great times. I left 6th class and started high school which was just around the corner from home. I loved doing things with my hands so I done,metal work wood work and art, loved playing sport at school. We played cricket football,and also I played it of a weekend. I loved going to school I had a couple of girl friends. When I was 13 one saturday morning mum dad and myself,went to look at some boats. We went to a boat show and mum and dad bought a 16 foot carribean open run about. We had a caravan would,go away about every 2nd weekend. Dad would tow the boat up,and mum dad and myself would go fishing for whiting. We would buy 5 dollars worth of blood worms got 12 it was a bargain. And some days we would catch over 200 whiting,back in those days there was no bag limit. We had fun times fishing we would always have a good laugh. Also we would pump yabbies for bait, they were great bait the whiting loved them. Once you got a hit you new it was gone and had to re bait. Were blood worms the whiting used to push the worm up hook,so you got a few goes,it was great fun catching them. They were good little fighters, my mum used to bait her own line and take the fish off. She was a good fishing lady,there was one day we had this big march fly giving us some trouble. We had a fly swot so mum didn't stop fishing line in one hand and still catching fish and swot in the other we got it,well done to mum. They were great weekends away, we done that for a nume of years. Until mum and dad bought a block of land,and had a house built on it. So they sold the caravan and we still continued to come up for the weekends and holidays. Well I finished school in 4ᵗʰ form and got my school certificate, my mum was in charge of a supermarket. I was 16 and mum got me a job there filling selves packing peoples food and doing storemen work. Was my second job, while at school I got my first job saling newspapers around the streets and on main road. Done that of a weekend and I made some good tips at times. I enjoyed working in the supermarket as used to do different jobs,mum was a good boss to work for. Then I got my learners perment and dad started teaching me to drive. He bought this old vw beetle off one of his mates at work,for $200 so we done it up changed the color painted it blue and white. It was a great little car cheap to run,I remember when I got my license. I was going down this step hill and the brakes failed lucky that I was able use the hand brake. So I was able to get car home driving slow,and using the hand brake. Dad was able to fix it, my dad was a very clever man. Before we got our big boat mum and dad bought a little fiberglass dingy and dad made a out board motor,of an old victor lawn mower engine mad all the leg shaft and propeller. It went well and if you wanted to go in reverse you just turned it around. I ended up getting a apprenticeship as a fitter and turner,for 4 years. And was to do with trucks. The factory had about 300 workers it was a good place to work, there was a couple guys. That I used to hang around with out of working hours,one was a member of a bike gang. And they used to have party's, they excepted me I had a holden panel van. It was only because I was friends with guy from work. One night they had a keg and it was $10 for your share of the beer. And they made a rule the first person to fall asleep,would get wet on. And that person was me they put me in one of those big old lounge chairs that you sink in. And they said you want a smoke of a joint,I said no but in the end I tried it. First time they set me up,you guest it I was first go to sleep and woke up with water running all over me was not nice, I never went back to that big shed. I was a member of a panel van club, name mid city van club. Thats were I met a girl which became my girl friend. I went up to the coast about twice a month,we would have bbqs go to pub and just hang out. Some weekends we would have panel van rans,were we would go for a drive somewhere. We would have panel van shows they were great times. Then back to work on mondays after leaving that job went and worked at island on harbour as a fitter. That was only for a short time, then I got a job at a warehouse. As a forklift driver storemen, which was close to home. After leaving there I started work at markets, at company johns as a forklift driver packer. We filled orders for stores starting time was midnight 12 to 8am,it was a good paying job. Then we would go to pub across the road have a couple of beers and some games of pool and then go home. That was for a period of time,then got a job driving tow trucks working for towing.Was not a good job as you had to get in cars put gear stick out of gear,and tie steering wheel,after people were taken to hospital.

Went to some bad smashes, continued going up to the entrance of a weekend it was only about one and half hours traveling time. It was a lovely area there was a lot to do there,some weekends would back van up to a railing on the lake. After a night at the pub if you had a hang over, I would open tail gate roll out and take 2 steps and I would be in the water. Didn't worry me if it was winter or summer, it was a good way to sober up. As I was growing up I used to drink at a few pubs near were I lived And loved playing pool,of a saturday and friday nights. Some people would play for a beer if you won. Would stay on table and get free beer, and it could be singles or doubles it was a good way to saved money,if you were able to win. And some nights we would go to epping club and play snooker for free,back in those days the schooners were only 40 cents. So you could have 5 for $2 thats cheap. Now there about $4 to dear to drink at pubs. It's getting close to my 21st birthday which was to be at my mum and dads house. They were buying a couple of kegs, and hiring a dance floor juke box, the big day was fast approaching. My girl friend and I had talked about when we were going to get married. We had not told anyone,girlfriend was planning on telling her parents the weekend after my 21st and same for me. The big day has arrived some of my friends came around to take me up to the pub Mum told them not to get me drunk he has a big night a head. Well they ordered this big mug held 6 schooners, I managed to drink it then we had a few more beers. I had to go to the toilet when I made it in there,I forgot to step up. And fell over straight into the troff hands into the water was not nice. One of my friends came in then went out and told the others, so they were all there having a laugh. And I said is anyone going to pick me up so we went out to the bar and they were trying to sober me up. I arrived home to get ready for my big night, and tried to walk in a straight line and look ok for mum. Was not to be what did I tell you I said mum it's a big day,she said just go and have a shower. I felt better after the shower people started arriving. Mum said there was about 100 guest coming, The garage was set up with a few tables. For all the food and there was enough to go round. And the bar was set up the duke box was pumping great songs. You could pick the songs you wanted what a great idea.We had one 18 gallon and one 9 gallon keg plus half a dozen magnums if champagne. People were arriving family and close friends had arrived,the weather was kind to us,we had a big tarp set up from the boat port to fence just in case it rained. And the food was all catered for, mum and dad done a great job bringing it all together. Someone had given me a full yard glass, and they had it filled up for me. I had a few mouth fulls of it,and no more I want to see the night out and have good memories, your 21st is one of your special birthdays. More people had been arriving they had a table set up for the presents. Everyone one was having a great time,we were just waiting on a couple more people to arrive. Then food would be served the people that were doing the catering. Had done all the set up of food was great. It was good that mum and dad,were able to relax and enjoy them selfs. Food was served at 8pm, there was heaps to go around. Food was good everyone said it was nice,desert was served two to pick from. As people were finishing up,it was time to cut the cake and make a speech. There was a big timber 21st key with cake that mum and bought. Mum and dad were standing along side of me, I cut the cake and people were clapping and saying speech speech. I was handed a schooner from a mate. I surprised myself how well I spoke, thanked mum and dad the catering people. And thank family and friends for coming,and continue enjoying your selfs. As the key was past around for people to sign.I think I got up on stage with mum for a dance. Then I needed another beer,I had that and couldn't see girlfriend. So I went looking was not out the front of house, not at the back. Went in the house to find her in my bed room on my bed with a best friend. I was in shock just couldn't believe it, Then will opened his mouth I said shut before I shut it for you, told him to get out of my sight. Why I said again she said not what you think,I don't want to hear it thanks for wrecking my night. Did you forget we were going to get married as I'm crying and tiers running down my face. Get out leave me alone just sat on bed and had a good cry. I went in bathroom threw some water over my face, and went out to find a mate. He gave me a envelope with a couple sticks in it, so we went out to my van to have a good smoke, he wanted to know why I was so wild. I just caught her in bed with my best friend that was going be best man at wedding. So he went home dad was in garage when I was walking down drive, I said you want a beer dad he said none left, both kegs were empty. So there was 2 bottles of champagne so we opened one if them. Dad said cheers not nice after drinking beer,finished glass mum said time for bed time was 2am. I had 3 friends staying in my bedroom, when I layed in bed started thinking about earlyer. And I was pleased I went to sleep, then hear knock on door it's mum. Do you boys want bacon and eggs no was our answer. She said come on you will feel better don't think so, it was ok but didn't make me feel any better. So I went to van to have a joint I felt a little better but the pain was still there. Had a coffee then we started to clean up. Then I sat down had a look at key there was no room left on it,was a lot of names. It was going to be a long day of pain, which I had for 19 years. Well my story continues this is were I become 1 and 2. One was when i was straight, and two when I was stoned or drunk to escape the pain. But life had to continue all I could think of was my 21st night. 2 people wreck that for me. Well it was back to work at midnight on monday night at johns at markets. There was a couple guys that worked there that used to take these little tablets to stay a wake. I asked if I could have a couple just to get out of it. The truckies took them stay a wake. And I felt good. That night shift is finished so we always go across the road for a few beers,and play pool before I go home. While I was there I called john a friend, to see if I could score of him. Called in on the way home he said so sorry to hear your news of your 21st. And I just burst out crying I calmed down,I had a smoke while he made up a mix, so we had a few cones and I felt good and laughing. I bought 2 blocks of hash. We continue having a laugh while he done some work on his bike. He said any time you want anything just give him a call. That made me feel better knowing I can score when I want it. I said good bye went home, had a shower and some food and bed. Back to work had a couple of cones before leaving, felt good I talking to a mate while at work. He said do you want to come to a party on Saturday A lady owned the house,they called it the dive. Had a great night there was a few people there, everyone was having a great time. It's amazing how different I felt after having couple of beers and some cones,the only problem is it doesn't last and you come down. It was sunday morning didn't feel good, so I had a beer and couple of cones. Starting feel better now monday was fast approaching. So the pain continues and life goes on, back to work. During the week I was in contact with chris the biker. See if I wanted come to another party at the dive I'll be there. It's saturday here we go again, I meet two navy guys. They were off the heads on herion, one of them asked if I would swap 2 sticks for a hit of herion. I kept saying no no no,they were not listening to me, and I was afraid that I would become addicted to it. I was just happy smoking grass and hash. I was feed up with them asking me,ok but don't give me the same you have. As they use it everyday, they put the belt on my arm. And couldn't find the vain, I said just stop forget it. They told me to shut up then they found it,once they took belt off,I rushed outside side and was sick then started dry reaching. I wentdown pub working so I raced down there,I was telling her over the bar. And this old guy grab hold of my shirt threw me on the floor and started kicking me.june jumped the bar pushed him off me what are you doing,he said took me back to her house kicked the navy guys out. And she stayed with me till I was better,she was a great friend,and I never touched it again.It was sunday afternoon I felt better so I decided to go home for a rest,and see mum and dad, sat out in our sunroom and sat there for a while. Had tea went to bed. Woke up the next morning still thinking of my 21st, I don't think I will ever forget that night. I was thinking I need a brake from my job try something new. I new a guy that worked for a transport company, went and saw him. He saw his boss told him what jobs I'd done, he gave me a casual job washing prime movers welding and repairing gates of the trailers,and going out with drivers to help load trailers then we would go to weigh bridge,make sure the weight was right over axles. As when you go interstate you need to be weighed, at weigh stations. I had a chance to go with one of drivers,he was going to western australia the following week. Went home and told mum and dad,might be good for me to get away. So I left my job and told lady in house. She said having a party on saturday so I went to that,I needed a brake from this place as well was making it my last time. You would not believe it and some of his mates turned up from bike gang. They ask me if I new any women to in vite, so I went to pick her up,they took her into a bedroom. And then I heard screaming and she ran out of house screaming rape. With in 15 minutes the police turned up and the bike gang told me to tell a pack of lies. And we got taken to the police station, I feared for my life so I lied to the police,they said my story is not the same as others. And looks like I was going to be charged with rape,I said I wasn't even in room. I said call her grandmother she will tell you it's happened before. Police said it all checks out and your free to go. All could think of I need to get away,so I phoned said will come to western australia. When home packed my bag said good bye to mum and dad,I thought I would be away for about 2 weeks. That was not to be when we were going along the nulabor we ran over a kangaroo and it went bang,with in seconds there was this rotten smell in cab. I used nearly full can of brutt deodorant, we arrived in perth there for a week or more. And we got a cruiser and runabout to take to the gold coast,we called into a service station at southern cross. To fuel the tanks up and have a meal met up with some truck drivers he new. They gave him a container of pills,that keep you a wake. Now our long trip across the nullabor begins,he gave me couple tablets. It took us 4 days to get gold coast. We unloaded the boats and met up with one of the guys from our yard. He was heading back to sydney,I said can I come with you. I had enough of being on the road and wanted get home.

Took us 12 hours to arrive in sydney,we unloaded and I went home. It was so good see mum and dad, what an experience that was never to do it again. Had a few days rest, went and saw my mate mick. And scored some hash had a smoke with him, have missed that. He ask where I had been, western Australia queensland. I need to look for a job, I managed to get a job with a transport company, picking up containers and general freight off the wharfs. It was a great job I really enjoyed it, and I was able to have a smoke when I wanted one. I remember one day I was sitting in a rank waiting to pick up a load. I had a block of hash in the truck and 2 custom officers walked, past the truck and they had a sniffer dog. With them and the dog started going off. And the customs officer just pulled on the dog and said come on how close was that I said to myself. I remember that day so clearly because the freight my boss had asked me to pick up. Really needed 2 trucks I went and phoned him,to tell him he said sky's the limit. What do you mean he said just keep going up ok I said. I said to the fork lift driver just bring it all to the truck and what I have. The clerk said your mad you will have to leave some. So all the solid freight went on the tray of truck,then started putting rest on top. Had 4 pallets left so I said I will unload them,and put them over top of load. I said to myself this is crazy I tied load down the best I could. As I was driving out of shed everyone I past were looking at me. It was a slow trip back to the yard,when I got out of the truck. Went got boss when he saw it, he said how did you get all that on. He came down and had a look, he said great job now I know what you meant by sky's the limit now. my boss said don't put that much on again. When I would get back to the yard I then had go to shipping companys, get paper work for next days work. It was a good paying job with lot of over time. And I could afford $100 a week spend on pot, I met a couple of drivers there they also smoked one was a dealer. So I had another person I could score off, I loved working there was great driving trucks you was your own boss. It was even better when days I would be picking up containers,and take to company's to unload. The days you would start early you would get breakfast mony and if you worked back you would get tea money,so on pay day which was fridays. You would get envelopes with breakfast an tea money plus your wage not bad I say. Just up the road from yard we drunk at the hotel, I worked fo this company for 7 years, and most days I would have a smoke if hash grass or heads. Everyday I carried the pain of my 21st, one afternoon after work mate said come over my place. and have a smoke, so we were having a couple of cones. And there was s knock at his door mate said it's my dealer. Which he forgot was coming he said who's this. He's a good friend which I only just met.this guy sits down pulls a gun out and puts on the table. Oh no I said to myself he opened this bag pulled out a big slab of black putty hash. Wow I said This guy said make a mix while I cut these up into 1 once blocks. Which was 28 grams at $380 a once. The smell was over powering,we had our smoke andmate said take this for your help. Was about 6 grams of hash,that made me very happy. So my days continue get stoned to escape the pain. An other weekend had arrived I picked up 2 mates and we went for drive to buy a bong. They had a few to pick from, so I found one had a spill tray around it. And got a couple of cones we went back to have a smoke we were down at the boat ramp. Just about to mull up and heard bike pulled up along side of us and it was a policeman. This is not good tried to hide stuff, one of mates had his hash in tin and put under back wheel. He radioed for back up.Police car had arrived they were searching car found new bong hadn't even smoked out of it. And found my stash, so we were put in police car taken station. One of the officers said your bong is the best one out of all them. I was charged with 3 offenses and 2 mates with 1. And we were due in court the following month. I was afraid I would go to jail so told mum and dad, mum said if you want smoke it do it in your bedroom. The day had come go to court I was charged $50 for each one,got off light which was good.The other 2 were fined $50 for 1 offense. It was for a drink so we went to the pub for a few beers. And some games of pool. A year had passed with new job, and I had 2 weeks holiday. So mum and dad and myself,went to forster to the caravan. For some time to relax and go fishing in our boat,most times we would come back with a good feed of whiting. We had some fun times together,I loved staying in caravan, we would have a few beers and dad would light the bbq. One day we went looking at blocks of land,and mum and dad found one. They liked and bought it and had a 2 storey house built on it,and had a in ground pool put in. As they would retired there when finished work. With us going up there for a while I got to know a few of the locals,which became friends. It was great to get out of sydney for weekends and holidays. The pub was my local drinking hole, when mum and dad and I. First came to forster mum and dad were the 2nd people to book into for holidays, it still stands today. We stayed there before buying the caravan. Well the holidays were just about over 4 days to go, on a saturday morning I met up with some friends. And they said have you got your key ring for the lucky cartoon draw,yes my number was 57. Year I was born it was up to 7 cartoons,you guessed it I won. So we had a good drink that night. 3 of my friends lived in house on point road, it was called the goonie club. The next day i invited me to a party, had a 11 gallon keg port bourbon couple buckets of oysters and heap of meat for bbq. Was $20 ahead nothing like a good party. The day after some sore heads had 2 days left, before our holidays are over. But we will be back looking forward go back to work. Always hate leaving it was a good brake, got back to work the boss said. You have a new truck coming until then he said you will be driving one of the ford bogies, and I said yes alot of container work. It was a great job some factory's when arriving they would say,have know one to help you. But you will be looked after there was one place they imported lobster tails. So they would give you half a dozen tails. I remember one year the boss said we have 40 containers to get off glebe island container terminal. And there had been a strike he said your dad works there can help us to get them off, with out lining up. I saw dad he said would be ok told my boss, and he gave me 2 large bottles of scotch for dad. Comes in handy when you know someone,as each day would go by. I still had the pain so most days I would have some cones in truck. You know I was crazy there was always that chance would ran into customs,as happened already. You never new when they would show up on the wharfs or depots. First week back of holidays it was friday afternoon,and looking forward to the weekend. Some of us drivers used to hang out at the local pub till 3pm,then go back to yard. So you would not get another job. Well I got back and there was a truck loaded with rolls of paper.boss said to me take this to botany,thats all I needed. I started to check ropes he said there ok, when I was driving up missiden road camperdown. I had never forgotten this day I heard this car with the horn going and it was load,my first thought was a roll of paper had rolled off truck. And landed on the car when I got out of cab,saw this half a ton roll rolling across the road, and went in between 2 parked cars. Thank you god no one was hurt I rang the boss. He said anyone hurt no I said. Told him were it was and he told me to continue to botany to unload. In the mean time 3 drivers went to pick it up in the ute. I arrived back at yard 5pm so much for early finish. Arrived home had shower some tea,told mum was going out. to get drunk and stoned, what a week it has been. This was a cycle every weekend get drunk, and everyday get stoned. This pain I was suffering just would not go away,only when I was drunk or stoned.I would feel good and happy,you would think it would not affect you as much as it has for me. I'd say we all handle things different.Well another saturday has arrived phoned a mate went down to his house, we made a mix then we went to local hotel. For a few beers and some games of pool, some people were arriving. And we would play for a schooner, so if you won you would hold the table and drink for free. Most times my mate we would win, we played alot so we were good. Sometimes we would get knocked off it's all part of it. We used to go to rsl, and play snooker on the big tables and it was free. I loved playing it there was some skill to it. Most sundays you dried out ready for back to work on mondays. After a while my boss would ask me start early to go sit on ranks, then we would have to wait for wharves to start at 7am. It was good doing container work,as when it rained had no tapping up. I remember at darling habour there was a pub,across the road from the wharfs and would open at 3am. And thats were most of the wharfies would be,some of our drivers used to go in have a drink.The next day the wharfies went on strike, wanted more money. They were on strike for over a week, so we still had some work to do. We had freight in yard and some containers, that we could deliver we had work for that week,I remember this as it was yesterday.boss said we could leave at lunch time friday, and monday spend the day washing the trucks. On tuesday morning I was called up to see mate he was reading the local paper. He said I want you to go 126 point road and see a young lady and say my boss has sent me here. To pick up a load on I was driving a long the road. And they were terrace houses saw number had a red light out the front. I've been set up but I still go in, knock on door and this beautiful lady open door. I said I have to see lady she shouted out to her, told me to sit on lounge. Lady that was on lounge started rubbing my leg then one that open door sat close to me.lady came down said can I help you. Yes my boss has sent me here to pick up a load so they all had a laugh. And this man said whats going on, so I tell him he said go back and tell your boss. You won't get a load of my girls there all clean. So I called into the yard told boss father, he said go and see the boss In the mean time he called him, got up in the office he said what happen told him everything he had tiers running down his face from laughing. Couple of drivers said you should of had lunch there and booked it up on him put joke back on him. They all had a good laugh,least I got 2 legs rubbed, got more than he did. Well the wharfies are still on strike. We just got word that the wharfies are going back to work, so were going to be very busy,as the shipping company's paper work never stopped. We were still receiving that everyday. boss ask me if I could do some over time picking up containers from the wharfs. So I was getting home late and leaving early next morning, to sit on ranks. While waiting I would have a few cones,done this most days when sitting in truck,waiting to be loaded. And I would think of the extra money I would get, so I was able to by double of hash. So life was good I enjoyed driving trucks, but still had the pain of 21st which I will carry for the rest of my days. It got a little better when stoned or drunk. It's friday afternoon been a busy week, just arrived home mum still at work. Dad is home we start to get ready for a weekend away,looking forward to it we loved going away Mum and dad would be retiring soon to the bay, and I will move up in a few years. We arrived to stay in new house, it was 2 storey house on corner block with a in ground salt water pool. We went fishing the next morning, mum dad and I always had fun fishing together,have great memories of our times together fishing. Well we caught over 200 whiting again,it would take us a while to clean them. Dad made a fold up table and we would go to a beach across the other side of bay. We would put table in sand stand in water to clean fish,mum would give us a hand. Was a great little spot plenty of sand, for a swim at high tide and we would have picnics there as well. We where enjoying the new house, it's always sad when we have to leave go back to sydney. Mum and dad would have happy hour most afternoons,dad brewered home brew,he would have a large bottle. Mum would have a scotch,and I would have a couple of stubbies. It was not long until mum and dad would be retired, and move up. Well it's monday start of a new week, when I arrived I had go up see peter. Told me that he is driving you to homebush to pick up the brand new truck isuzu. I could not get over it I had only been with the company for 3 years. Don't you just love the smell of new car or truck. It even had air conditioning radio lay back seats, was going to be great driving it, put a smile on my face. I thank my boss he said just look after it,I said I would but was not going to be responsible if someone else drives it. My life was changing and I will be moving into my own place,all I could think of was party time. I had enjoyed living at ryde with mum and dad had some great memories. And 21st night was the worst, mum and dad I went up to shops to buy a new fridge for my unit. When we came out I said to mum were is my car,it had been stolen and there was a mazda rx7 left in it's place. I yelled out and a security guy came over,he radioed police. They turned up and they said the rx7 was stolen on the friday. Told them car was locked and steering wheel lock was on. They said we don't like your chances of getting it back.Two weeks had passed I asked mum could I please have a loan of your car. When down to see a mate to have a smoke,when I pulled up in his drive. He said were is your car I got it stolen two weeks ago,he said I saw it parked out side block of units. I said come on lets go,arrived there and it was still there. Not a thing wrong was locked up,fishing rods still in it. I said I will drive it back to your house,you drive my mums car. Back to mum and dads, drop mate off at his house. And went to police station, told them found car. They said were is it we need to finger print it. Told them it's out side, they went off at me. You should of left it and called us,I just wanted it back. Get out they said and I went home, happy days. The next night I was to take this girl out for first time,she worked were mum worked I met her parents she said come on lets go. Went to a restaurant food was good plus great company, I said to myself could this be the one. I needed some happiness, we hit it off. It was 4 years past 21st. We went out a few times we enjoyed each others company, we made love one night. She said have you thought about getting married I said yes. I said how about you,her answer was I want to marry you and have 6 kids. I thought oh no what are you going to do. I will stay home and look after the children, and while I work two jobs. What have I got myself into,need to think long and hard about this. Start of another week of work I was enjoying driving new truck,I kept thinking what debbie said. Well it's been another busy week all I could think of,was will have more to spend on drugs. And at the pub on the sunday I thought I would trade panel van in on another car. Went to a yard l high performance cars. And got a GTS monaro 308 hz,color was british racing green. And had bathurst mags,it was a nice car. I got home and said to mum and dad,come and have a look at my new car. Mum said what have you done, I got it on high perches, and the interest was sky high. Mum said we will go to the back,mum got a bank loan. Payed the car yard off,then I payed the bank. Which was a much better deal. It was so nice to drive and it had some power. Some sunday nights we would all meet at shop on parramatta road,then go down to benelong road. And they would have street drags,had some good nights there and not so good. Couple times the police closed the road,and there was only one way out. So it took a while to get out,if you were nice to them and answer questions. They would say don't want to see you here again, did that stop me. No it was a thing we done some sunday nights. One night I thought I would have a race,there was a girl that had a ex police car. Was a lime green charger, and she left me for dead,I was still in first gear as she went passed me. That was the end of my racing,they were good the old cars. You could work on them change plugs points, spark plug leads change oil filter plus oil. Not like the new cars today, this day arrived home from work. I was not even out of car guy across the road said this is my car, I don't think so he said my car was stolen and this is it. How about you look at the rego, no it's not my car and stormed off. Didn't even say sorry, I had been thinking was time for a change,and move to forster. I was not fussed on marrying and having 6 children. And was fed up with the drugs taking them everyday, and bad memories needed a new start. I gave my noticed were I worked I loved that job. The following weekend I went up to the bay,tell mum and dad. I need a new start I'm moving up to the bay. Was able to stay with mum and dad,till I got a place of my own. I got a job at joinery,told owner still in sydney. Moving up in 2 weeks said come and see me. I thanked him that he was giving me ago, never done any spray painting I could learn. Don't we all love moving and packing not. Well I ssid my good byes,and was looking forward to a new start. But I still could not escape the pain of 21st. I started at the joinery which was a 2minute drive,nice and handy. I was enjoying the job, I had always enjoyed doing things with hands. And one day a week I delivered vanitys, on the central coast and sydney. Well it was my first weekend,living at forster, mum and dad and myself. Went looking at caravans found one at fleet street, had some money in bank, it was enough I had always enjoyed the caravan life style. The rent a week was cheap $63 and I was five minutes from work and my parents. It was close to pub and club and shops. Friday nights at pub were great, and you could not help to see the dealings. That went on so was not long until I was smoking drugs again. I new 3 guys that I could score off,and had a good credit rating. So I could get it on tick and pay at the end of week. I became friends with a guy in the park and he smoked. He had a brother that lived in sydney, which sold drugs plus speed un cut. So that was another person,there was no escaping. So I was quickly back to getting stoned everyday again, now I have place of my own. Would have cones when I arrived home from work,and have a few cones before work. And when I was at work I would go out to car,have lunch and a few cones. To get me through to knock off time,as I was still carrying pain of my 21st. When I would get home have a few cones and 2 stubbies then go to the pub. My dad used to make home brew I had a plastic box,it carryed 8 long necks. And I would have them every week as well. People had no idea that I was stoned as my eye's where the same every day. One thursday greg that lived in park, came and saw me. Asked if I wanted to go to his brothers on Saturday he is having a all night party yeah I'll be in that. When we arrived I met his brother and a few other people he said have you had speed before a couple of times. So we had a couple of lines few cones.

then a few beers as more people were arriving. It was about midnight now and know one seemed to be going home. I said to greg has your brother got a room I can go sleep. So I went to have a sleep was not to be,with the music still going people laughing,and morning was fast approaching. I managed one hour sleep, I went out to lounge room some people still partying. Old mate gave us some breakfast, I wanted to leave about 10am head back home We managed to leave at lunch time,driving along the f3 to newcastle. I looked across greg was asleep I thought I would like some sleep. I was so tied I put window down to let fresh air in, I could feel myself starting to go asleep, which I did lucky I ran over those lane devider bumps and I woke up. Pulled over for a break had an hour sleep old mate said he would drive. He was worse than me, well we got back on the road. Finally made it home dropped mate off and said see you later,I went straight to bed. Was not looking forward to work,I was surprised I was ok the next morning. I had a full day of under coating panels doors then bake them. Take them out of booth sand them, and paint the next day. The day went so fast,I arrived home to relax had a few beers and a few cones. Old mate came over and gave me 1 gram of speed, I said what's this for. He said for taking him to Sydney, I needed it like a hole in the head. But I kept it and thought it's just something else I can get out of it on. So I started making snow cones. I was looking forward to the next weekend big old mate ask me if I wanted come to party at anna bay. It was friday afternoon we finished work at 1pm,so I go straight to club. Get my wages go and have a schooner,then on way out call into bottle shop. Buy a cartoon bag of ice,go home put beer and ice in esky. Have a few cones and 3 beers,then walk to pub. To get drunk and have a great time I would do this every week. Then go to club on way home and have a few bourbons. Then walk home. It's saturday party time to start the day off few cones couple beers start to feel better. So I drived us out to the party, they had a keg started drinking was talking with girl a very good friend. She said come out on the deck,there was a few guys. Resting on the railing so I joined them,was only there for couple minutes. And the rail gave way and I fell back forwards,saw legs up in air. Was about 12 foot fall landing on sand and some concrete rocks. I heard someone said call a ambulance,girlfriend came down you ok yeah I'm alright. Went to get up she said say there till ambo comes,I was busting go toilet. She said I'll get a blanket and milk bottle,I said don't worry the bottle will over flow. The ambulance had arrived he said I hope the christ you can walk as I'm not carrying you. He put me on stretcher the first corner he went round I shot off and onto floor. When we got to the hospital he open doors up,and said what are you doing down there. I said been there since first corner, I had exrays doctor said. You are very lucky only that you are drunk you didn't brake your back or any bones. Just your going to be very sore for a while. He was not wrong it was the only time I was glad that I was drunk. As you have read up until now since my 21st, my life has not been good. But as people say life goes on and you will get over what happen. Was not to be only when I was stoned or drunk I was happy. Everyday was the same day in and out,but I continued getting myself wasted. Even thow I moved from sydney the only thing that had changed in my life was. I lived in a different area. Some of my friends worked on the osyters, and they would drink port when at work. One of them had a 30 foot punt with a 90hp out board. There was a weekend we went up the lakes, for a day of drinking. They were great times up lakes the water was so calm, the punt would never go past pub,with out pulling in to stock up on beer smokes and food ice. Sometimes we would have the portable bbq, and cook up a feast. We had a couple of car bench seats in the punt so we had the comfort as well. They were long days so most sundays I would make it a rest day and no drinking. Just have a few cones a guy I worked with he would come

in see me on the saw cutting draws,and have a laugh.
And see my eye's say you've had some bongs again, yeah
I have he kept asking me to come to church I said no
way. No I'm not coming to church.so I just continued
doing what I had been doing for 18 years. I remember
one christmas party we had at the joinery, the boss got
a few kilos of prawns plus cartoons of beers. I lost count
how many beers I had,I was standing talking to some
work mates. Started eating prawns they were big
prawns,I have always sucked the heads. I was sucking
one everyone was saying how grosse. One of them was
sick on one of ladied shoes from office. I was told to
stop I said save them for me, will suck them later. People
started leaving I thought good time for me go home.
On way home I called into see mum and dad, when
leaving said see you tomorrow. I was waiting to make
a right hand turn,and a police car was coming towards
me. Must of seen how blood shot my eye's were,so I
turned out looked in mirror and he was turning around.
I parked car got out and went into a neighbors house
down back yard. And he sat down the road waiting for
me,I walked across road told mum and dad. They said
leave your car here and your dad will drive you home.
When dad was driving me home he was still there
waiting for me. He will have a long wait,arrived home,
made up a mix had a few cones and a beer. And as I do

most nights fell asleep in chair. It was morning had to do some last minute christmas shopping, left car at mum and dads. It was christmas eve done what I normally done,had some cones and beers. And walked down to the pub, to have a few more drinks. When I arrived home later that night I tripped on front step,and I couldn't open door. The lady next to me came in and said whats wrong,I don't know what happen to keys,I was sure I had them in my hands. So we went for a walk she said have you fallen over on way home,not that I remember, no luck finding them. Arrived back home she shined the touch on door,there they are she said. They were hanging on steel bar half way up screen door, I thanked my neighbor for help,and got inside at last fell asleep.Its Christmas morning have another shocking hang over, went had a shower starting feeling a little better. Before I left for mum and dad's had a few cones and a beer. Arrived at parents ready for a great day with family,mum said you look like you need a swim. Good idea mum so I went for a swim, dad came and joined me. The pool was good for a hang over, more family were arriving. Got out and dressed ready for a big day, every Christmas mum and dad would have family over. It was time to open presents best part I think,once we had finished. Mum would put some picks out,then it was time to start drinking. Loved our times together with family they were always big days. Plenty of food and drink,well that was another Christmas day gone. They come as quick as they go, then it's boxing another day of food and drinking. We had some great times at mum and dad's house Well I'm on holidays for 2 weeks,so planing on going out fishing in our boat with mum and dad. We used to pump yabbies it was hard work, or we would buy blood worms. They were 5 dollars a dozen,we would always catch a good feed of whiting,we used to buy blood worms off some frieThey were my aborigines friends that live on a island they were great friends. We enjoyed our fishing we have great memories. While I was fishing I was off the drugs and beer. We would give some fish away to friends and family, there was always to much for us. We just enjoyed the time together as a family, and the whiting were great fun to catch. Mum would give dad and me a hand to clean them,that was the worst part about catching them. Mum and dad bought this toboggan, for me to get towed behind the boat. There was one day we were over other side of the bay, near beach,and I fell off into a big school of big brown manaors jelly fish. And they stung me all over my body,and I was yelling and screaming. I could hear mum saying he's been taken by a shark. They quickly came over and pulled me into boat,your alright mum said no I've been stung by those jelly fish. I never rode it again. There was hundreds of them in the water, they were every where. Went dad started the boat up and took off, you could feel them getting hit by prop. There was no way of missing them, that day we had a bbq nothing like fresh fish cooked on the bbq. Dad and I would have a couple beers as they cooked,and mum would prepare the salad. The following weekend was dads 70th birthday on saturday night. Mum and I had arranged a 11 gallon keg as a surprise for dad. Before dad left to go and play bowls,at club. gave me a job to do, was make sure I put his bottles of home brew in his beer fridge in garage. And told me make sure your mum doesn't put any food in it,ok dad you can trust me. We had a guy from the club come around, and set keg up as it needed to be settled down. Then mum and I continued get things ready.Dad arrived home from bowls,he said did I take care of his beer. Yes dad we had half a dozen bottles of home brew in fridge. I said to him come out near the pool,I will buy you a beer. Dad was so surprised what a great idea he said. Poured him a beer it was perfect, so we had a beer. Then he went and got changed. Ready for a big night of family and friends,I was at the keg most of the night. Pouring drinks It started pouring not so good,and you always get the experts I'll fix it. I said leave it alone the cellar man said not to play with it, just give it a rest for a while. And it started pouring good again,people thought it was a great idea. And works out cheaper than cartoons. Was time to cut the cake and blow out candles, I'd made a plague from timber had engraved happy 70tn birthday day. It was painted with two pack paint and gold letters. Dad loved it, we had it hung up in garage, the night was coming to a end. Everyone had enjoyed them selfs,the next morning there was about 3 gallons left in it. The neighbour across the road, Charlie and betty had invited us over. So we took keg over to finish off They were good neighbors to mum and dad. I said my good byes as I was back to work on monday. Arrived home had a bbq for tea, couple of beers and some cones. I had been hanging out for some cones,since friday you get used to having it every day. Well it's monday start of a new week,need to start day off with some cones. And every day I would say to myself, when will I ever get over this pain. As I've said before my life could of been so much different. Getting stoned every day,and drinking most days. And getting drunk of a weekend, it's only temporary so you start all over again. Be days were I would run out of heads grass hash,and have no money to pay day. Because I had a good credit rating,I could score any time. Had about 3 dealers if one didn't have anything, I could always get it off someone else. When ever I got some good heads, I would save the seeds and plant them. The plants were never as good as what I would buy, but it was free smoking. One of the dealers ask me if I wanted to sell for him,I thought this was great. He had putty black hash at the time and he gave me some blocks to sell. I never sold them I'd keep them so I had heaps to smoke. It was not a good move, but I had a problem and it just started to get worse. As the days weeks months years went on,I kept saying to myself I need help. I didn't want to tell mum and dad. but my problem continued everything had just become a habit. I felt so good when I was out of it,I was so happy but everyday the pain just followed me. A couple of years has past since my dads 70th birthday, and things are still the same with me. Still working smoking drugs and drinking ever day. A couple of weeks was my mum's 70th birthday,and we are going to port macquaire for the weekend. My aunty and one of my cousins lived there,we left early The hardest thing for me is when I'm with mum and dad,I'm unable to have cones. When your away so I look forward to it when I get home, We arrived and jeff took mum down to the town ship, and bought her a soft serve ice cream. It was pouring with rain jeff said are you ready to get your feet wet. said we have booked you a ride on a para flight. Were you get towed behind the boat, mum's replie was not on your sweet life. He had mum going so we went back to my cousins, had a few drinks the ladies had scotch and the men had beer and we had some picks. There always good had to go past chicken in the biskit cheese dip. We were going to one of the clubs for mum's birthday dinner, we always enjoyed going up to port. As we had my cousin and auntys place's to stay,plus my other cousins would be there, Was great catching up with them,as we don't get to see each other now.As we have all gone our different ways. So it was always special when we met,and have a laugh.The only thing wrong I think is the time goes so fast. It was time to get ready go out, we arrived at the club to celebrate mums 70th. The food was lovely a good selection, beer was good. It was great to catch up with the family, we all had a good time. I went to bed when we got back to cousins house. It was a lounge pulls out to a bed,every time I rolled over I could feel a steel bar. So I didn't get much sleep. We left early sunday morning called in to get fuel,and went to McDonald's for breakfast.We had a good trip home,I was looking forward to my bed. Couple of beers and some cones,now I was feeling better. Back to work on monday,next party was my 40th which we are having at mum and dads. Looking forward to that the boss came and saw me,will you be ok to go to drive over night. So I had to work a full day load truck in the afternoon. Go home have a shower get changed and get on the road,for 7 hour trip,was not looking forward to it.I was passed sydney on the hume high way,had the cb radio on listening to the truckies. It's a busy road I was having trouble staying awake. So I pulled off to the side of the road, got out of truck had a walk around. I was feeling better so I resumed driving, just went through goulburn. And the police pulled me over for breath test that was all good,so I continued I was approaching the federal high way. The road is wide there hume 2 lanes and federal high way 2 lanes. This is were I fell asleep behind the wheel for maybe a second. Heard a noise and woke up that was not good. So I found a pull in bay and thought have a couple hours sleep,no bed in truck had to lay across seat. Not real comfortable managed a few hours sleep. And got back on road to be at my drop off point by 7am,arrived had a smoke coffee bit of a rest. Then we unloaded truck got paper work signed,then I was off back home. Would of been nice to go book into motel for the day,but I had to be back at work that day. So you work the hours out from monday 8hr day then drive to canberra 7.5 hrs driving. Pulled over for 3hrs then trip home 8hrs with 3 hours sleep for 2 days not good. Arrived back at work told boss that was total madness what I just done,lucky to be alive. So I explained to him his answer was I'll get someone else. And to do what I done yes was his replie,I said to him it was only that I have had a history of truck driving that I'm back here save. And you going to put someone in that has done little driving. I said the only way to do it save is to book into a motel,and come back the next day so thats what he done,so I continued doing all the drving. I loved driving out in the open air your own boss.Well it's been a busy week, so first thing go to club get wages cartoon of beer bag of ice. Go home put beer ice in esky,now for shower couple beers some cones. Then walk to the pub for a great night, this was my usual thing each weekend. Just get totally wasted as each day that goes by,I still suffer with the pain of my 21st. Then after night at pub and club, I would stagger home have some cones then go to bed. Each morning would wake up with a shocking hang over,so I would have a few beers and cones for breakfast. Then have something to eat couple more cones then back down to the pub,for a day of drinking playing pool. I was begining to think I need a change,but I would just keep thinking. Bad habits are hard to shake so I just continue doing the same old thing. Work 5 days have 4 beers each afternoon up to thursday and cones morning at work night. Then get drunk friday and saturday nights what a life.Then sundays I would dry out sobber up ready for work again.Some friday nights I would hang out at the club, the guys that lived there was were good friends. And we would have oysters 20 litre bucket, as they worked on oyster leases. And we would have port beer spirits, we had great times it was close for me to walk home. We had big partys there would go for two days. We had old lounge chairs car seats had a big double shed down the back,big bbq which was used alot. Was a timber one when we finished cooking,take plate off and put more timber on. To keep warm in winter I remember one night.Pete said you don't need to walk around the street way,he took a fence post out said there you go. Now you have a short cut home,as I lived in caravan park at back,so it was handy for me. Well another weeks work a head, so it all starts again I'd have half dozen cones before going to work. I just couldn't give up I was addicted, and just haven't been able to give up. I kept saying I need help but I was happy getting stoned and drunk,and when I wasn't I would be un happy. My 40th birthday is coming up soon so I was looking forward to that, I have been enjoying my job as I would drive truck 2 to 3 days a week. Started going to central coast one day sydney. Which would be over night trips,then same thing weekends do the same thing. Get drunk and stoned. I remember one night coming home from the pub,thought I would walk home along the beach. Than walk on footpath not something I done often. I got to the park and saw the slippery dip,that looked good for a rest. So I sat down leaned back and fell asleep. Had no idea how long had been there, and a person was pulling on my arm. I said piss off leave me a loan, then this voice said it's the police. What are you doing he said I'm drunk and needed a rest,and went to sleep. Were do you live he asked in bee street,so they gave me a lift home. That was nice of them I'll stick to the footpath next time. Well it's a week to go before my 40th,bring it on I said. I had a big esky that I bought to hold more beer, so I will be testing it out. I saw a dealer during the week and ask him to hold on to a bag of heads for me. And he said I'll do you a good deal for your birthday so a got 1 once. I arrived at work on the thursday,and boss said I want you to take a load to canberra come back friday. I really didn't want to go but I went, all I could think of was my party. So I took a little bit of heads and papers, to have on trip. Well I've unloaded now to fuel up have some breakfast,and trip back to port stephens. Driving back on the hume high way,there are always the big semi trailers. Flying past me and when empty you need two hands on steering wheel,to stop truck moving about in lanes. Well thats another week over now time for my 40th party saturday night.And I get wasted again,shower get changed then down to the pub for usual friday night. Had 4 beers at home and some cones, I was pressing bottle top lid on my head. And I forgot about it I arrived down the pub,and everyone was laughing at me. I said to the bar maid whats wrong with everyone, she could hardly talk. I went over to table and my friends were all laughing, whats the joke I said. No one would tell me until I went to get another beer, and different bar maid said take that bottle top lid off your head. I forgot all about it.Well that's another night over at pub time for walk home couple more beers and cones then off to bed. I've been thinking for a while now, I'm over this getting drunk and stoned every day. Each day is the same get stoned and drink and get drunk friday saturday nights. It's saturday birthday party day, as I do most saturday morings start drinking and have cones. Went around to mum and dads get eskys ready full of beer's. Sit things up weather was not good was pouring rain,so it's going to be in garage and dad would be cooking on bbq.Well it was starting out to be a great night,friends were turning up and family members. And I had one thing on my mind,I needed to change my life after this night. And I felt this was going to be the last time I got drunk. So I was making sure it would be a great night, the beers were going down well. The picks are always good with beers, mum and dad were doing a great job. The tables were set and the bbq was ready, don't you just love the smell of the cooked steak onions. The food was beautiful great company, then the cake came out. Blow out the candles made a speech,told everyone to enjoy them selfs. The beers were going down well, I said to a work mate those beers have to be finished tonight. It was a good night said to there was 2 beers left,gave him one and I had the last. I was happy they were all gone,people were saying there go byes. I thanked mum and dad for a nice night. Friends wife was giving me a lift home, when I got home I had half a dozen cones went to be. Woke up sunday morning with a shocking hang over. So I made a mix had some cones and breakfast,sat in lounge chair. Thinking about my life and I needed to change,well it was back to work on monday. Its was start of new week rob one of my work mates came over to say hi,and laughed your stoned again yeah. He said again we are praying for you at early morning prayer,I said thanks told him I need help. I'm over the life I have been living,and been thinking about suicide. I have be come fed up everyday, day in and out is the same. Getting stoned drunk when I could. There would not be a day go by were I would not be stoned. As if I had no money I could always get my drugs on credit. That's another weeks work gone,and it's friday night. My dealer I was buying my drugs off,was thinking of seeing him. And ask for some herion to commit suicide. I new there was a better life for me,and new there was a God. And i got down on my knees and cried and cried out too God for help. I had tiers flowing down my face like rivers. And my neighbor was knocking on the door,yelling out are you ok. I went to the door sorry for disturbing you I said I need help. Whats wrong I said need help,she came in told her all about it. I said if it was not my love for my mum and dad, and what it would of done to them knowing there son committed suicide. And I love them so much I know there was a better life. Told her I'm going to church on sunday, I called rob that had been praying for me. Tell him I will be at church on sunday,he said thats great you can sit with us. It was sunday morning I was having second thoughts,no I'm going see what it's like. I arrived out side there was so many people, and I saw rob went in with them. It wasn't to bad rob took me to see the pastor. He was pleased to see me,sit down we sing some songs then he said do a message,then open the altar for prayer. The pastor opened the altar and I went up,I was standing there with all there's other people. I could hear people crying and the pastor praying for them. Someone came up behind me and said extend your arms out while he put his hand on my back.The pastor came to me,and ask me what was wrong. Told him I was sick of life and had thoughts of committing suicide. And said I need help I need a change, he asked if I believed jesus died and rose again,yes he told me was going read the sinners prayer. And I repeat after him and ask if I wanted to be baptised in the Holy Spirit yes. So he was praying and I was crying started to shake,and fell backwards snd hit the floor. I heard this voice what happen pastor said you was touched by the Holy Spirit. I stood up and he gave me a hug,and others came to congratulate me. I felt different then I needed to sit down. And a lady came and said to me now the next step,was to go into the waters of baptism. This was all new to me I said, rob was the pastors name. He arranged for me to see him during the week.I meet the pastor on thursday afternoon after work,he ask me what I thought of church. I enjoyed it told him all my story he spoke to me about the water of baptism. I told him I was still smoking drugs,he said it affects people differently. Some people get delivered from drugs and getting drunk. And others when they go into the water of baptism, get delivered the old is dead the new is born when you come out of the water. A month had past and meet with pastor talk more about my baptism day.said have you been drunk since I was baptised in the holy spirit that was huge for me. As I used to get drunk every week,and I have not been drunk since. My baptism in the holy spirit on my first sunday at church,praise God that my life is changing. I have been enjoying church have meet some nice people. This week I'm to meet with the pastor to talk more about my baptism day. You wouldn't believe it I had come down with bronchitis, I said I still wanted to get baptised on my set day. Pastor said no we will wait until I'm well,ok I said as it was winter at the time. And the water will be like ice,a month had past and I was well again. And the date was set 19th of july 1998,I ask mum and dad would they come. Would make the day all that more special having mum and dad there. The day was fast approaching and I was so looking forward to it,I just new God was going to do a miracle on that day. My life has changed so much, have stopped getting drunk and only been stoned a few times. That is a miracle in it self, I had been telling family and friends about I'm now able to talk in tongues as I have the Holy Spirit dwells with in me. There probably saying he's mad, no just praising God my life is going to change even more. Bring it on I say been counting the days down for my new life to begin, and to be free of drugs and getting drunk. I have 7 days to go and it will be sunday I was so happy. Well its sunday morning a big day for me,and It was freezing still winter and a strong westerly wind blowing.

The pastor had announced that there is a baptism after church today please come down and support phillip. It will be at conroy park I was so excited,rob my work mate he will be coming into the water with me and pastor rob. We had arrived at the beach there was alot from church, and I was so happy that mum and dad were there,I new God was going to do a miracle in me. It was so cold the pastor told me what was going to happen,then the 3 of us started to walk out into the water. They had hold of each arm and down I went under the water. And out again put my arms up in the air,praising God that I was a new person. The old phillip gone the new is born the pastor and rob gave me a hug. Then others were hugging me,and mum and dad. Went to toilet get out of wet cloths, I was so happy a new lease on life. And I never touched the drugs again or got drunk. Praising God that a new person was born,I continued going to church most sundays. 17 years has past and to this day never touched the drugs or got drunk again,praise god only he can do that. Still enjoying church there was so much more,that I could of put in this story. But I felt was best to leave out,I pray that this story will change others. That are experiencing what I went through. 27/09/2015

Printed in the United States
By Bookmasters